MW01593392

Message To My Daughters
The Ways of God by Nicole Atkinson

Printed in the United States of America

ISBN 978-1512050103

Unless otherwise indicated, Bible quotations are taken from the King James Version (KJV) – public domain.

Biblegateway.com © 1995-2010, The Zondervan Corporation. All Rights Reserved.

www.nicoleatkinsoninc.com

Messages to my Daughters

"The ways of God"

This book is written to every little girl/young woman in the world. Especially the two gifts Jamiya & Janel whom God has so graciously put under my care. As I look over my life and the decisions I have made I often contemplate how my life would have turned out if I knew the will of God at an early age. I made the decision not to dwell on the past, but to make it my mission to teach, train, guide and to be a living example for young women everywhere.

TABLE OF CONTENT

Proverbs 31:30 Favour is deceitful, and beauty is vain: but a woman that feareth the Lord, she shall be praised.

Jamiya & Janel

I HAVE BEEN CHARGED TO LOVE YOU

You are a gift from heaven sent to prosper

under my care. From the moment God

revealed to me you were conceived I vowed

to love you. God has entrusted both of you to

me and with every ounce of my being I will

ensure your safety. Making it my primary

goal to create an atmosphere for you to grow

and flourish in the power of God. I have a

responsibility to highlight the gifts placed

inside of you. I seek the Lord daily for a

vision concerning how to raise and nurture

you to the best of my ability. Nothing can

compare to the joy of parenthood and I thank

you for choosing me. I vow to honor and

respect you and to teach you the ways of God. With God there is unlimited possibilities. You have been given the keys to fulfillment in life and they will open ALL doors destined for you. Jamiya and Janel, _____,

_____ (just in case the Lord blesses me with more it still applies) we are on this journey together. Let's enjoy this life always putting God first and trusting each other every step of the way.

Chapter 1

~YOU ARE A GIFT~

Psalm 127:3 Children are a gift from the LORD; they are a reward from Him.

No matter what anyone tells you, you are a gift from the LORD. The purpose of family is for us to produce and multiply. God has placed you under my care and together we can express God's love in the earth. Since you are a gift you must understand how special, unique and loved you are. Not only in my eyes but in Gods eyes as well.

If you can imagine how much I love you God's love is a trillion times greater. It's so great that it can't be measured. He blessed you long ago and allowed time to catch up to send you to your dad and I. Now it's our responsibility to nurture, love and care for all of your essential needs. As we seek God for ways to instruct you it shapes the foundation for your future.

Everyday I pray for your welfare. I want you to know how important you are not only to me, but also to the world around you. God has made you to shine in this world. If at any moment you don't feel like your capabilities are enough just remember a King created you. You are the daughter of the Most High. He has a throne you know where He invites us in daily to spend time with Him so we can get to know Him. O how great you are in His sight. Whenever we receive presents we are excited and trilled to know what's in the package.

Children are an extension of the Lord as the scripture states, "Children are an inheritance from the LORD. They are a reward from him." (Psalm 127:3, GW). You have been left with me to continue with the same characteristics imbedded in you from God. Since you are my child it is my responsibility to have my life in order so I can raise you to the best of God's ability through me.

My prayer everyday is for God to continue to build your father and I up in His word so we can take care of the gifts we have been given. When we come face to face with God He is going to ask, "How did you take care of my children".

Having this responsibility I know and understand every one of my decisions will impact your today and your future. I will be selfish enough to yield myself to God so I can hear from Him on how to encourage you as my daughters.

Isaiah 49:15 (NIV) "Can a mother forget the baby at her breast and have no compassion on the child she has borne?

<u>*Mother and her daughter relationship*</u>

The bond between a mother and child is a unique one. As God has crafted us together through the process of reproduction a mother experiences internally what a father cannot. At the onset of pregnancy mothers have a connection with the child as they grow in their womb. Mothers are able to experience a connection before the child enters the world. This is the same connection God has with us and He teaches mothers how to nurture and care for their children.

At this point I only have two daughters so I can only speak to the relationship of the mother and daughter. God uses the analogy of a mother's bond being unbreakable when He asks the question, "Can a mother forget the baby at her breast and have no compassion on the child she has borne?" This analogy displays the importance of a mother's role in a child's life. It is the responsibility of the parents to ensure each child has adequate care.

Every decision parents make should incorporate how the results will affect all parties involved especially their children. Children come into the world depending upon parents and guardian's to establish a support system. It is my charge as a mother to safeguard the welfare of my children.

We know children learn through nurture and nature. The home environment and social environment play a major role in the development of a child. It is my goal as a parent to ensure their greatest source of influence is that of godly character. A child's greatest source of influence should be that of the parents and guardians way before any television star, peers or outside source.

I know I know there are a lot of young woman who are not fortunate enough to have godly influences in their lives at the moment; but don't stop there. God is able to place people in your life to help nurture your path. There are a lot of parents who lack knowledge and unfortunately their children are not being raised in a godly environment.

If you find yourself in this place begin to pray immediately for people of godly character, integrity, wisdom, knowledge and who are filled with the Holy Spirit to enter your life. As a mother it is my goal to make sure my children are well taken care of. I will display compassion in all areas of their development- spiritual, emotional, through education, and all social aspects. Every component of my child's life will come before God in prayer.

It is through a relationship with God where we are able to find the strength and power to raise our little girls to become woman of virtue. Spiritual and moral development begins in the home. Since our children are gifts to us it is our duty to care for God's packages to the best of our ability. God has given us something fragile, unique and filled with His godly character in the form of a child to raise and nurture.

The best way to know how to develop the best mother and daughter relationship is to follow the example given by God and to display His same characteristics of love. Here are a few scriptures of support to encourage the love of God.

1. *Psalm 144:12 King James Version (KJV) 12 That our sons may be as plants grown up in their youth; that our daughters may be as corner stones, polished after the similitude of a palace:*

2. *Proverbs 22:6King James Version*

(KJV) 6 Train up a child in the way he should go: and when he is old, he will not depart from it.

3. *1 Peter 5:2-4English Standard Version (ESV) 2 shepherd the flock of God that is among you, exercising oversight, [a] not under compulsion, but willingly, **as God would have you**; [b] not for shameful gain, but eagerly; 3 not domineering over those in your charge, but being examples to the flock. 4 And when the chief Shepherd appears, you will receive the unfading crown of glory.*

Psalm 144:12(NLT) May our sons flourish in their youth like well-nurtured plants. ***May our daughters be like graceful pillars, carved to beautify a palace.***

Our children are the masterpiece of God. Since God has given us daughters we are required to ensure we cultivate them to embrace the design God created. As a mother I am tasked with providing you with the necessary tools to produce a character of moral excellence.

As you grow and develop you will mature into a woman of virtue, one who is pleasing to God. As I raise you my instruction will help you live as the beautiful daughter God predestined -His gorgeous piece of art. When the world sees you they will see an extension of God.

The Bible says you'll be like *graceful pillars, carved to beautify a palace.* Your character will embody the very essence of God. Your mannerism and actions will reflect godly standards. Those who come into your presence will recognize your character and conduct as one who has been refined by God Himself. Each day you will grow in the attributes of God.

Your palace is God's earth. You have been sculptured to decorate the earth with your life. It is my job to help you see your worth by impressing upon you how important you are.

If you obey my instructions from God your life will become a blessing to the world through what you do for God. The world will become better because of you.

Proverbs 22:6 (KJV) 6 Train up a child in the way he should go: and when he is old, he will not depart from it.

Worry will not live in my house in regard to how you will chose to live your life. I am confident that by teaching you the knowledge of God you will never depart from this teaching. Even when bumps appear in the road, I know you will have Gods, "still small voice" inside of you to lead you back home.

Training is a process and will take time and commitment to show you the skills necessary to live a God- filled life. Don't be discouraged God continues to teach me every day. Through this process we learn what God requires, His desires and how to enjoy the life He has given you.

As God's children your entire life is a training process. Stay close to God and He will guide you in His perfect path. (Psalm 48:12 For this God is our God for ever and ever; he will be our guide even to the end.)

Peter 5:2-4 (ESV) 2 shepherd the flock of God that is among you, exercising oversight, not under compulsion, but willingly, as God would have you; not for shameful gain, but

eagerly; 3 not domineering over those in your

charge, but being examples to the flock. 4 And

when the chief Shepherd appears, you will

receive the unfading crown of glory.

This is so important for parents to understand as God has given us authority we must take our position as a Shepherd to the flock God has placed in our care. Not to rule them with an iron fist, but with the love of Christ. Where discipline is required we can administer it through love and issue appropriate consequences for irrational behavior.

God is a God of humor. Often times I

find myself saying things to my kids like "stop winning, you don't have to cry to get your point across." God immediately convicts me and says, "You do the same thing daughter, have mercy".

Or when our children don't listen to our commands we get out of whack and demand respect. Again God immediately convicts me saying, "It takes you five times over to obey my voice, have mercy." One day while God was convicting me for my unjust correction of my children He showed me a comparison between our relationship with Him and the relationship we have with our children. He went on to explain how we easily get upset and disappointed when our children don't follow our instructions because we are guiding them with their best interest at heart. We are instructing them to accomplish things that will only produce outcomes beneficial for their well-being.

Frustration sets in because we want the best for them but they aren't living up to their fullest potential so we get upset. God said plain as day, "My intentions are the same, and again have mercy".

IT'S MY RESPONSIBILITY TO SEE YOUR GIFTS AND TALENTS TO PREPARE YOU FOR YOUR KINGDOM ASSIGNMENT

Judges 13:8 -10 8 Then Manoah prayed to the Lord and said, "O Lord, please let the man of God whom you sent come again to us and teach us what we are to do with the child who will be born." 9 And God listened to the voice of Manoah, and the angel of God came again to the woman as she sat in the field. But Manoah her husband was not with her. 10 So the woman ran quickly and told her husband, "Behold, the man who came to me the other day has appeared to me.

The angel of the Lord appeared to Samson's mother before he was conceived. The angel spoke to his mother instructing her to submit herself to the Lord because she was about to conceive a child from God. The woman was so excited about what the angel of the Lord told her she immediately ran and informed her husband.

Her husband Manoah prayed to the Lord to send the man of God again so he might receive the same instructions as his wife. God listened to Manoah and the angel of the Lord appeared to them again. In this moment of visitation Manoah asked the angel ""Now when your words come true, **_what is_** _**to be the child's manner of life, and what is**_

**his mission**?" (Judges 13:12).

I believe Manoah had a relationship with God and this allowed him to receive this awesome revelation. He understood God's principles as it pertains to raising children. It's important for parents to seek God and receive instructions on how to propel their children into their destiny.

This is exactly what Manoah did. He turned and petitioned God for instructions for the welfare of his child. At this point Samson had not been conceived. That's how important children are to God. He has plans for them before their parents ever come together. It is my responsibility to pray for you as my child. I NEED to seek God for instructions on how to raise you in order for you to be prepared for the assignment God has created you for.

Everything God creates has purpose. As your mother it is my job to seek God on your behalf. God gives clear instructions on how to create a nurturing environment for you to grow and develop into the woman God predestined you to become. When God thought to design you He had a specific job for you to complete on this earth.

Your gifts are what God needs you to use in the earth to bring glory to His name. As your mother I will help you discover what those gifts are as God reveals them to me. It is imperative for your father and I to stay before God in prayer to continue to lead you into your destiny.

Don't ever be afraid of what God has created you to accomplish. We all have assignments we must fulfill for the kingdom of heaven. Different times in our lives we will be tasked to accomplish things that seem impossible. And that's okay; it was never our responsibility to fulfill God's work apart from Him.

As we yield ourselves to God He works through us to shine His light in the earth. Make it your daily duty to devote yourself to God and ask "how may I serve You today." As God teaches me I'll teach you how to seek

God for yourself. Your relationship will grow and develop to a place where you will no longer depend on me to show you God, but you will seek Him for yourself. My most important job is making sure you know who God is.

IT IS MY REPOSIBILITY TO BE A LIVING EXAMPLE

I would be a fool to try to instruct you in the ways of the Lord if I myself were not a living example. Am I perfect "NO", it is my heart desire to try my best to be a woman of godly character—YES!!!. When you look at me you will be able to see Jesus working through me. (Now when I fall short remember to show mercy!!!) Not only is it my responsibility to be an example to you, but you are also an example to me.

No matter what your age is God works through you. Knowledge and wisdom are given to those who receive it. I try my best to live my life in a manner that is pleasing to God and in return will be pleasing to you. Don't think for a moment that parents are perfect and have it all together.

At times parents yell too much, are quick to judge, and fail to listen. There are many days where the Holy Spirit convicts my heart and I find myself in Psalm 51 asking God for forgiveness.

PARENTS MAKE MISTAKES. In my mistakes I will find the time to say, "I'm sorry." Nothing in life will be a smooth journey without hiccups. As we walk in God, He will show us where we need correction and discipline. We will make the necessary adjustments and continue in God's strength.

Just as you are growing daily I am growing daily as well. I make it my business to seek ways to better equip myself in order to be the woman of God you can look up to. As a living example I believe the Word of God and apply it to my life. I am living everything we will discuss in this book or have made the mistake and pray you will not make the same ones I did. As God teaches me, I'll teach you and vice versa.

PRAYER FOR OUR CHILDREN

~1 Chronicles 29:19 (KJV)~ 19 And give unto Solomon (put your child's name here) my son a perfect heart, to keep thy commandments, thy testimonies, and thy statutes, and to do all these things, and to build the palace, for the which I have made provision.

~Luke 18:15-16 (KJV)~ 15 And they brought unto him also infants, that he would touch them: but when his disciples saw it, they rebuked them.16 But Jesus called them unto him, and said, Suffer little children to come unto me, and forbid them not: for of such is the kingdom of God.

~Isaiah 59:21 (KJV)~ 21 As for me, this is my covenant with them, saith the Lord; My spirit that is upon thee, and my words which I have put in thy mouth, shall not depart out of thy mouth, nor out of the mouth of thy seed, nor out of the mouth of thy seed's seed, saith the Lord, from henceforth and for ever.

~**Proverbs 3:1-2 (KJV)~** 3 My son, forget not my law; but let thine heart keep my commandments: 2 For length of days, and long life, and peace, shall they add to thee.

~**1 Peter 2:9 (KJV)~** But ye are a chosen generation, a royal priesthood, an holy nation, a peculiar people; that ye should shew forth the praises of him who hath called you out of darkness into his marvellous light;

~**Ephesians 5:1(KJV)~** 5 Be ye therefore followers of God, as dear children;

~**Psalm 112:2 (KJV)~** 2 His seed shall be mighty upon earth: the generation of the upright shall be blessed.

~Genesis 18:17-19 (KJV)~ 17 And the Lord said, Shall I hide from Abraham that thing which I do; 18 Seeing that Abraham shall surely become a great and mighty nation, and all the nations of the earth shall be blessed in him?19 For I know him, that he will command his children and his household after him, and they shall keep the way of the Lord, to do justice and judgment; that the Lord may bring upon Abraham that which he hath spoken of him.

~Psalm 147:13 (AMP)~ 13 For He has strengthened and made hard the bars of your gates, and He has blessed your children within you.

~Proverbs 1:8 (KJV)~ 8 My son, hear the instruction of thy father, and forsake not the law of thy mother

~Proverbs 4:1(KJV)~ 4 Hear, ye children, the instruction of a father, and attend to know understanding.

~Deuteronomy11:18-21(KJV)~

18 Therefore shall ye lay up these my words in your heart and in your soul, and bind them for a sign upon your hand, that they may be as frontlets between your eyes.19 And ye shall teach them your children, speaking of them when thou sittest in thine house, and when thou walkest by the way, when thou liest down, and when thou risest up. 20 And thou shalt write them upon the doorposts of thine house, and upon thy gates:21 That your days may be multiplied, and the days of your children, in the land which the Lord sware unto your fathers to give them, as the days of heaven upon the earth.

~Genesis 12:2-3~ 2 And I will make of thee a great nation, and I will bless thee, and make thy name great; and thou shalt be a blessing: 3 And I will bless them that bless thee, and curse him that curseth thee: and in thee shall all families of the earth be blessed.

~Acts10:2~ A devout man who venerated God and treated Him with reverential obedience, as did all his household; and he gave much alms to the people and prayed continually to God.

~1 Samuel 1:11~ She made a vow and said, "O Lord of hosts, if You will indeed look on the affliction of Your maidservant and remember me, and not forget Your maidservant, but will give Your maidservant a son, then I will give him to the Lord all the days of his life, and a razor shall never come on his head."

~**1 Samuel 1:27-28**~ For this boy I prayed, and the Lord has given me my petition which I asked of Him. 28 So I have also dedicated him to the Lord; as long as he lives he is dedicated to the Lord." And he worshiped the Lord there.

~**1 Samuel 2:26**~ Now the boy Samuel was growing in stature and in favor both with the Lord and with men.

Chapter 2

~Jesus~

John 17:3 And this is eternal life, that they know you the only true God, and Jesus Christ whom you have sent.

Jesus is the Son of God sent to the earth to give us eternal (existing forever) life. God's original intent for mankind was for us to dwell in open fellowship with Him forever. Sin (disobeying God's will) entered the world and caused a separation between God and man (Genesis 3). God being so loving sent

His Son Jesus to the earth to redeem us back to Him.

Through Jesus we have been granted access back into God's presence. It is God's plan for you to know Jesus Christ by accepting Him as your Lord and Savior. In knowing Jesus you will know God. Jesus is the ONLY way to God (John 14:6 Jesus saith unto him, I am the way, the truth, and the life: no man cometh unto the Father, but by me).

In order to receive salvation (Deliverance/Freedom) you have to believe God sent Jesus to the earth to die on the cross and on the third day He rose from the dead and now sits at the right hand of God.

In order for you to receive forgiveness for your sins (anything contrary to God's commands) a sacrifice had to be made. Jesus became a living sacrifice and died on the cross for you and I. (Romans 4:25; 1 Peter 2:24).

(Romans 10:9 because, if you confess with your mouth that Jesus is Lord and believe in your heart that God raised him from the dead, you will be saved.) If you are not saved and want to invite Jesus in your life as your personal Savior recite these words out loud:

Lord I believe you sent Your Son Jesus to die for my sins. I believe He died on the cross and after three days

You rose Him from the dead and He now sits with You in Heaven.

If you say this prayer and believe you are saved. Now it's important to find a local Bible teaching church and become a member so you can grow in God.

As Jesus walked the earth He taught His followers everything God taught Him. Jesus only did what He saw God doing and only spoke words from His Father. (John 5:19 GW Jesus said to the Jews, "I can guarantee this truth: The Son cannot do anything on his own. He can do only what he sees the Father doing. Indeed, *__the Son does exactly what the Father does__*). Jesus is our living example. He came to show us how to operate as children of

God. His life shows us how to have a relationship with God and how to fulfill our purpose in the earth.

Apart from God (Jesus) nothing we do will matter. We can follow the example Jesus gives us in the bible to understand our position in God's kingdom. Jesus illustrates our relationship with Him in John 15. Here He describes Himself as the vine and God as the vinedresser and we are the branches.

As we are connected to the vine we are required to produce fruit (God's goodness in the earth). Anything connected to God / Jesus by nature will produce greatness (The purpose; will of God). It is our kingdom position to function in Jesus as branches of the vine. Staying in close communication with Jesus as He cultivates us will enable us to prosper in the earth. Our ability to grow and develop according to God's commands brings Him glory.

Before I began to walk with God I would have never been able to write books offering people the message of hope. Sure there are people who don't know God who publish millions of books. But if what they are doing is not God's plan it is meaningless. God revealed my gifts and talents and gave me clear instructions on how to accomplish His strategic plans. As I stay connected to the vine I hear from God and my actions produce favorable fruit and He gets all the glory.

It is important that you commit to studying the life and ministry of Jesus to develop His characteristics. *John 15:4-5 Abide in me, and I in you. As the branch cannot bear fruit by itself, unless it abides in the vine, neither can you, unless you abide in me. 5 I am the vine; you are the branches. Whoever abides in me and I in him, he it is that bears much fruit, for apart from me you can do nothing.*

The bible says in *(Hebrews 12:2 Let us keep looking to Jesus. He is the one who started this journey of faith. And he is the one who completes the journey of faith. He paid no attention to the shame of the cross. He suffered there because of the joy he was looking forward to. Then he sat down at the right hand of the throne of God.)*

Having this knowledge of the great sacrifice Jesus made for you will compel you to honor and obey God. Jesus walked the earth having to endure every form of temptation you will encounter throughout your lifetime. Instead of succumbing to the pressures of the world He kept His eyes on God and remained focused. Following Jesus is the greatest accomplishment anyone will achieve in life.

John 10:10 The thief cometh not, but for to steal, and to kill, and to destroy: I am come that they might have life, and that they might have it more abundantly.

Jesus came to show us how to live in close proximity with God. His life was an example of the freedom you have in God. You can look at the world around you; people need the freedom that Jesus offers. People are committing suicide from stress that God never intended for them to bear.

Wars are breaking out because of pride, hate, and selfish ambition. Murders happen daily because people don't know who they are in Christ. Jesus is the message of hope. He died to free you from the pressures of life. This does not mean you are exempt from facing hardships. What it means is you can endure in His strength. Being in Christ you have authority over the enemy. You can live your life in peace by giving your problems to God. Allowing His power to lead you.

Jesus teaches you how to live the life God created you to have. God's original intent for mankind was for us to live life in abundance having dominion over the world He created. *(Genesis 1:26 And God said, Let us make man in our image, after our likeness: and let them have dominion over the fish of the sea, and over the fowl of the air, and over the cattle, and over all the earth, and over every creeping thing that creepeth upon the earth.)*

Sin entered the world and distorted God's plan. Jesus came to uncover your internal strength given by God and to show you how to operate as God's child. Also to get you back into God's reality. God's reality is this --you are created in His likeness and in His image. By watching Jesus He will guide you in a life of freedom. Where you are free from lies of the enemy and are able to receive the truth that God created you to reflect His nature here on earth.

Let's look at this same scripture in The Message Bible:

Genesis 1:26-God spoke: "Let us make human beings in our image, make them reflecting our nature So they can be responsible for the fish in the sea, the birds in the air, the cattle, And, yes, Earth itself, and every animal that moves on the face of

Earth." God created human beings; he created them godlike, Reflecting God's nature. He created them male and female. God blessed them: "Prosper! Reproduce! Fill Earth! Take charge! Be responsible for fish in the sea and birds in the air, for every living thing that moves on the face of Earth."

When Jesus says He came that you may have life He is opening your eyes to the deadness you have if you remain in sin. For the wages of sin is death. *(Romans 6:23 For the wages of sin is death, but the gift of God is eternal life in Christ Jesus our Lord).*

In Christ you have received new life where you are able to experience God's presence through a relationship with Him.

This life is not some ordinary life but a more abundant life that is overflowing with the God's glory. When God called life into existence in the Garden of Eden He had plans of greatness for all of His creation.

Jesus came to refocus your mind from the world's systematic teaching back to the original thoughts prearranged by God your Father. Jesus came so that you could live an abundant life. A life without limits to the things of God; God has already blessed every area of your life. He commands you to prosper, reproduce and fill the earth.

A life of abundance is where you reflect God in every thing you do. Jesus's ministry reveals God's plans of an abundant life. As Jesus walked the earth He displayed his dominion and power over everything. He was in constant communication with God and was able to accomplish His purpose. Jesus was aware of His position as the Son of God and the power associated with being in God.

Jesus is teaching you how much power and authority you have when you surrender your life to God. His life ought to inspire you to accept your positon as one who contains the image of God by accepting His love and obeying all of His commands.

Some of the Characteristics of Jesus

Jesus is our friend

~**John 15:13-15**~ Greater love has no one than this, that someone lay down his life for his friends. 14 You are my friends if you do what I command you. 15 No longer do I call you servants, for the servant does not know what his master is doing; but I have called you friends, for all that I have heard from my Father I have made known to you.

Jesus is the best friend one could ever ask for. Whenever you need Him He is always there. As you grow in your relationship with Him you will feel more and more comfortable revealing yourself to Him. Although He already knows everything about you -Jesus wants you to accept His invitation as friend and enjoy communication with Him. He cares so much for you that He laid down His life so you could have a second chance at life.

Whenever you feel down and out Jesus is right there. Jesus is always available to talk to. He has compassion and cares for you because He can relate to you because He experienced the same life you are now living (Hebrews 4:15). In your relationship with Jesus you have someone you can trust. He has your best interest at heart. His friendship is built on the foundation of bringing out the best in you at all times.

He talks to God about you on a daily basis. He reminds God of all the good things they implanted in you. He prays for you and covers you from the evil in the world. There is joy in having a friend like Jesus. You don't have to live a life of confusion, depression, or stress. Jesus has overcome the world *(John 16:33 I have said these things to you, that in me you may have peace. In the world you will have tribulation. But take heart; I have overcome the world).*

Anything that weighs heavy on your heart can be given to Him and He will give you rest. *(Matthew 11:28 28 Come to me, all who labor and are heavy laden, and I will give you rest.)*

Key Elements of being friends with Jesus:

- Intimate connection

- Fulfillment

- Receive wisdom/ revelation

- Unexplainable Joy

Jesus is High Priest

~Hebrews 4:14-16~ Now that we know what we have—Jesus, this great High Priest with ready access to God—let's not let it slip through our fingers. We don't have a priest who is out of touch with our reality. He's been through weakness and testing, experienced it all—all but the sin. So let's walk right up to him and get what he is so ready to give. Take the mercy, accept the help.

Jesus is our Redeemer

~**John 14:6**~ Jesus said to him, "I am the way, and the truth, and the life. No one comes to the Father except through me.

~**John 3:16**~ "For God so loved the world, that he gave his only Son, that whoever believes in him should not perish but have eternal life.

~**Matthew 28:18**~ And Jesus came and said to them, "All authority in heaven and on earth has been given to me.

~Ephesians 1:7~ In him we have redemption through his blood, the forgiveness of our trespasses, according to the riches of his grace,

~John 1:29~ The next day he saw Jesus coming toward him, and said, "Behold, the Lamb of God, who takes away the sin of the world!

~John 1:14~ And the Word became flesh and dwelt among us, and we have seen his glory, glory as of the only Son from the Father, full of grace and truth.

Jesus intercedes for us

~**Romans 8:34**~ Who then is the one who condemns? No one. Christ Jesus who died-- more than that, who was raised to life--is at the right hand of God and is also interceding for us.

Jesus is a healer

~**Matthew 4:23**~ And Jesus went about all Galilee, teaching in their synagogues, and preaching the gospel of the kingdom, and healing all manner of sickness and all manner of disease among the people.

~**John 21:25**~ And there are also many other things which Jesus did, the which, if they should be written every one, I suppose that even the world itself could not contain the books that should be written. Amen.

Jesus is a teacher

~John 3:2 (ESV)~ This man came to Jesus by night and said to him, "Rabbi, we know that you are a teacher come from God, for no one can do these signs that you do unless God is with him."

The gospel Matthew, Mark, Luke and John give an account of the life and ministry of Jesus. The entire bible gives testimony about our Lord and Savior. What a friend we have in Jesus.

Chapter 3

~Holy Spirit~

John 4:26 But the Helper, the Holy Spirit, whom the Father will send in my name, he will teach you all things and bring to your remembrance all that I have said to you.

God is God the Father, the Son (Jesus) and the Holy Spirit. The Holy Spirit is the third person of God (His Spirit) given to you as a gift to reside in you. The Holy Spirit is your helper He helps you to remember the truth of God's Word and the works of Christ. The Holy Spirit lives in and reveals to you how you are to operate in God. The Spirit of God searches the heart of God and then informs you of what God requires. He is your friend who lives to teach you the distinct difference between what God wants and the things of the world.

Jesus did not leave you in this world alone. Not only did He give you the message of hope (The Gospel) He has also given you the gift of the Holy Spirit. The Spirit of God lives on the inside of you (1 Corinthians 3:16 Know ye not that ye are the temple of God, and that the Spirit of God dwelleth in you?) This is important to understand.

God is alive and active on the inside of you. God lives through you, you no longer belong to yourself, but to God. (You belonged to God all along) He is so kind he gives you free will to CHOOSE whether or not to allow the Holy Spirit to lead you in the things of God, which only led to victory. You have the option to continue to try things on your own.

I am sure you have already tried that and discovered it leads you nowhere. Why not allow His Spirit to teach you and show you the great and marvelous things God has predestined for you since the beginning of time. The Holy Spirit teaches us the attributes of God.

He examines our characteristics and helps us to function as a royal priesthood; God's elect people. (1 Peter 2:9 But you are a chosen race, a royal priesthood, a holy nation, a people for his own possession, that you may proclaim the excellencies of him who called you out of darkness into his marvelous light.)

The Holy Spirit is a deliverer of God's message. He searches the heart of God and then comes to deliver His plans to you. (John 16:14 ESV *He will glorify me, for he will take what is mine and declare it to you*).

Everyday you are faced with the choice to hearken to the voice of God. His Spirit within you will guide you on the right course for your life. The choice is totally up to you whether or not you will listen. It's important to understand pressure from outside influences will try to fight for your attention and try to persuade you in the things of the world. As a child of God you have to make a conscience effort to walk with the Spirit. Life will tempt you, as it did Jesus. You can follow Jesus example; when He was tempted He stood on the Word of God and allowed the Spirit to guide Him.

Anything contrary to the will of God comes from the flesh. The flesh is embedded in your sinful nature. Which Jesus died for you to be free from; God created you with purpose and with His guidance you will live an abundant life. He will guide, and protect you everyday on your journey with Him. Life abiding in God's Spirit is a life of freedom

You are free to explore the depth of God's great love for you. You yield yourself to what pleases God by listening to His voice speak from within your spirit. This kind of Spirit filled life opens your eyes to the covenant promise of righteousness (right standing with God).

Living in the Spirit you submit yourself to God's governing. His Holy Spirit only produces those things, which are beneficial for bringing glory to His name. Romans 6:20-21 clearly explains the distinct difference between walking in the flesh and walking in the Spirit *(**Romans 6:20-21 AMP** As long as you did what you felt like doing, ignoring God, you didn't have to bother with right thinking or right living, or right anything for that matter. But do you call that a* *free life? What did you get out of it? Nothing you're*

proud of now. Where did it get you? A dead end.)

You are not equipped to lead yourself

through a life that God created. God being so

generous has given you all things to ensure

you walk hand-in-hand with Him to maximize

your potential while you're in the earth.

(Galatians 5:25 AMP *If we live by the Holy*

Spirit, let us also ***WALK BY THE SPIRIT****. If by the*

Holy Spirit we have our life in God, let us go forward

walking in line, our conduct controlled by the Spirit).

Walking in step with the Holy Spirit is

evident and will produce the characteristics of

God in your life.

Galatians 5:22-23 But the fruit of the Spirit is love, joy, peace, forbearance, kindness, goodness, faithfulness, 23 gentleness and self-control. Against such things there is no law.

Chapter 4

~Faith~

Mark 11:22 And Jesus answered them, "Have faith in God.

Faith is another gift given to you by God. It is your ability to trust every word God has ever said. The bible says "Now faith is the substance of things hoped for, the evidence of things not seen." (Hebrews 11:1). As you live your life God requires you to trust Him in everything. This is where your faith comes into action. Faith requires you to believe the things you cannot see immediately with the natural eye, but you know it already exist because God has promised it to you in His Word.

You are not given a bad hand, after all you are being asked to trust the one Person who created all things and has power over all things. Exercising your faith shouldn't be hard because you are relying on God. He teaches you to have faith in Him at all times. God's promises never fail. God created the universe by faith and called you into existence by faith. We are just imitating how our Father operates.

(Hebrews 11:6 ESV) And without faith it is impossible to please him, for whoever would draw near to God must believe that he exists and that he rewards those who seek him.) When you fail to believe God you are not in a position to please God. Doubt and unbelief are a sure way to hinder your progression in life.

God doesn't place this limitation on you. He has given you the ability to believe beyond your wildest imagination and grab hold of the promises He has stored up for you. Faith gives you courage to get through every obstacle always remembering God is in control leading the way. Faith is a requirement for all believers to exercise on a daily basis.

Everything you do requires faith. When you wake up you use faith to get out of bed and to partake in your daily routine. God is trying to get you to fully comprehend the depth of exercising your faith by believing EVERY WORD that comes out of His mouth. Some things may seem impossible because of your limited human intellect.

It is extremely important to take the limits off of God and allow Him to manifest His Word. ONLY believe. Faith is the driving force for you to get what God has already predestined in heaven to become evident in the earth. God already has everyday prepared for every person He created.

You make the choice everyday if you are going to put your faith to work and receive what God has or allow unbelief to block what God is trying to accomplish. I hope you choose to believe God. (His way always works out better).

Everything in life requires faith. It took faith to write this book. I had to believe God instilled His vision in me. It was God alone who gave me the ability to write this book knowing it would be a blessing to millions of people around the world. My faith is constantly being exercised throughout this process.

The opposite of faith is doubt and unbelief, which produces fear. It's easy to fall victim to not operating in the manner God desires for your life. The enemy doesn't want you to receive all God has for you. What if I doubted God and allowed fear to keep me from writing this book? Not only would I be missing the mark with God, but millions of people across the world would miss out on the opportunity to know what God really thinks about them. Not only does our faith help us to believe, but it's also an avenue for God to produce His fruit in our lives.

As you live a life of continuous faith you will be in constant communion with God and He will be able to see His fruit manifested in your life. Faith gives you the ability to trust God and to complete every task He has assigned for you. This kind of faithful connection brings glory and honor to His name.

Faith is given to all believers. When you have examined yourself to make sure you have a clean heart you can ask God for anything according to His will and if you have faith YOU WILL RECEIVE IT.

Chapter 5

~Value Your Body~

1 Timothy 4:12 Let no one despise you for your youth, but set the believers an example in speech, in conduct, in love, in faith, in purity

As young women it is important to know how God commands you to control your bodies. Living in a society where sex is exploited in a negative way many young women are confused on how they should honor their bodies.

First your body is a temple, a scared building where the Lord lives. Knowing this it is imperative that you keep yourself pure from things that displease God and disrespect your body. God requires that you never engage in sexual activity outside of marriage.

Your girl friends might tell you it's the thing to do and little hot boys may try to seduce you. You are going to have to be strong in the Lord. You will grow in knowledge by understanding why God calls you to refrain from sex until marriage.

Your body is the temple where God lives. When you partake in sexual acts with a person the two of you become one flesh. The only person you were created to become one with is your husband. God doesn't place these commands on purity to keep you in bondage but to save you from the devastation associated with doing things contrary to His will.

God knows the hurt and pain that is associated with sex when used outside of the marriage covenant. When you have sex with someone there is an emotional attachment that continues long after the physical act has ceased. Marriage is a covenant agreement where the husband and wife make a commitment before God to be joined together forever until death.

When you have sex outside of this covenant agreement you and your partner are not committed to anything. The two of you can walk away at any time. Not to mention the risk of sexually transmitted diseases, or pregnancy that could occur. God called you to righteousness. Your body is worth far more than a little excitement.

You have to understand you are a kingdom citizen and in God's kingdom there are rules. These rules keep you free from the negative things that come from disobedience. You are not a robot who only listen to God's commands out of repetition, you listen and obey because you love God and want to honor Him with every ounce of your being especially our body.

God invented sex to be enjoyed exclusively during the holy union of marriage. As you grow and develop into a women of virtue you must learn to keep yourself pure. I'm not going to lie to you and make you believe I waited until marriage to have sex, because I didn't. What I can say is I wish I did. Reason being is because having sex releases a piece of you. A sharing of your inner being that you can never get back. God knows this and wants you to only share yourself with your spouse.

He also wants to spare you from the heartache associated with giving your body to someone and then it not working out and repeating the cycle over and over until you find the right person.

No one ever told me sex was something God wanted His children to wait until marriage before engaging in. I wish someone would have taken the time to tell me how important I was and that I am valuable. So I will say it to you, "YOU ARE IMPORTANT, AND YOU ARE VALUABLE."

Truth be told a man honors a women more when they know she honors herself. No man wants to date a woman who doesn't value her temple. Like I said before when I was growing up I was not taught the importance of honoring your body and saving yourself for marriage. My only lesson was I better not get pregnant.

There is so much more to your body and your purity. God holds you to a high standard. You are a queen in His eyes. Not just anybody can approach you and rob you of your purity. You belong to a King. Jesus paid a high price for you on Calvary. Honoring God with your body is a great honor and one that may not come naturally.

Pressure will arise from outside influences, especially from your peers who may be sexually active. You will have to make a choice to either succumb to the pressures of the world or honor God and receive the greatest reward, which is His blessing for your obedience.

Valuing your body goes way beyond sexual activities this includes the way you dress, how you conduct yourself and the value you place on having self-control. You have to see yourself the way God sees you. He sees you as the apple of His eye. You are His beautiful creation whom He created in His own image.

God sent Jesus to die for us while we were yet sinners because He saw the good in us despite what the world would have you to believe. God loves you so much He will do anything for you to grasp His love. Knowing this you have to place value on yourself. You were crafted and designed by the Almighty Himself; you know for sure how much value you possess.

You never have to compromise yourself for temporary attention or affection because God's love is enough. If you ever feel unloved or under valued consider God's love and all that Jesus gave up for you. His walk to the cross and death is an appeal to you that YOU ARE WORTHY. If you have already had sex STOP, ask God for forgiveness and keep yourself pure until marriage.

Hebrews 13:5 Honor marriage, and guard the sacredness of sexual intimacy between wife and husband. God draws a firm line against casual and illicit sex.

Scriptures

(1 John 1:9), (1 Corinthians 6:18),

(Hebrews 13:4), (1 Thessalonians 4:3-8),

(Romans 13:14), (Colossians 3:5), (Titus

2:12), (Psalm 18:24), (2 Corinthians 10:3-

5), (1 Corinthians 6:13), (Luke 11:34-35),

(2 Timothy 2:21), (Philippians 1:9-11), (1

Peter 1:13-16), (James 5:16), (Psalm

119:37), (Leviticus 20:7), (1 Timothy 5:22),

(Isaiah 60:1), (Titus 2:14), (Deuteronomy

22:15-29), (Genesis 2:24), (Hebrews 13:4),

(Hebrews 10:26), (Romans 12:1-2), (1

Corinthians 3:16), (1 Corinthians 6:16-19)

Prayer:

God keep our young woman in pure all the days of their life. You have instructed us keep our bodies holy, as You are holy. Reveal their true value and don't allow them to fall victim to the lies of satan. We declare they will not compromise their purity for anything. Show them how important it is to put you first in all that they do. When temptation comes we will thank You that for grace and always providing a way of escape. There is nothing to hard for you. Reveal to each of us how to honor our bodies and to keep ourselves pure in Your sight. In Jesus name we pray, Amen.

Chapter 6

~Purpose in Life~

John 17:4 I glorified you on earth,

having accomplished the work that

you gave me to do.

Purpose is the reason why you were created. God created each individual with a specific purpose unique to the gifts and talents He placed on the inside of you. Everything created by God is for His glory. It is your destiny to glorify God with your life. Our mission in life is to stay in constant communication with God to allow His Holy Spirit to direct your path.

As you draw near to God He will

nurture the gifts inside of you and lead you in pursuits to fulfill your maximum potential. God is always right by your side just like in everything you have to make a conscience choice to surrender your life to fulfilling his plans.

God has given me the gift of writing. When I was a teenager I fell in love with writing, I would write poems and would use writing as an outlet for my emotions. To me it seemed like a channel to express myself.

God was developing the gift He put inside of me to be used for His glory. Once I gave my life to Christ God inspired me to write books, and daily devotions to uplift others by giving them the message of hope.

This comes naturally for me because it is my destiny to reach people through God's Word. I have other gifts as well which God continues to develop and reveal to me.

You will have multiple gifts suitable for kingdom use as well. Your gifts are whatever you do naturally that brings you joy. Once your gifts are revealed to you through the Holy Spirit you are to utilize them for building God's kingdom.

Jesus is our perfect example of how to fulfill our purpose on earth. Right before He was to be persecuted He prayed to God letting Him know He fulfilled everything He was born to accomplish. God is pleased when we complete the task He created us for. Anything done outside of what God created us to achieve is a waste of time.

To let you in on a little secret God's plan is far better than anything we could try to devise for ourselves. There is joy in allowing God to fabricate every part of your life. His plans all lead to greatness and the fulfillment of His master plan.

(1 Corinthians 2:9-10 But as it is written: "Eye hath not seen, nor ear heard, neither have entered into the heart of man the things which God hath prepared for them that love Him." 10 But God hath revealed them unto us by His Spirit. For the Spirit searcheth all things, yea, the deep things of God.)

Your life is already written for you. God has prepared great and marvelous plans for you. If you obey His voice and allow the Holy Spirit to guide you, you will experience the beauty of what God created you for. God's plans produce righteousness. Allowing God to reveal His glory through you will show the world the goodness of God.

At the end of your life you want to be able to look God in the face and say the same words Jesus said, "I glorified you on earth, having accomplished the work that you gave me to do".

~**Colossians 1:16**~ For in him all things were created: things in heaven and on earth, visible and invisible, whether thrones or powers or rulers or authorities; all things have been created through him and for him.

~**Psalm 24:1**~ The earth is the Lord's and the fullness thereof, the world and those who dwell therein

~**Genesis 1:26**~ Then God said, "Let us make man in our image, after our likeness. And let them have dominion over the fish of the sea and over the birds of the heavens and over the livestock and over all the earth and over every creeping thing that creeps on the earth."

~Psalm 139:16~ (The Message) Like an open
book, you watched me grow from conception
to birth; all the stages of my life were spread
out before you,
The days of my life all prepared before I'd
even lived one day.

~Jeremiah 29:11~ For I know the thoughts
that I think toward you, saith the Lord,
thoughts of peace, and not of evil, to give you
an expected end.

~Revelations 4:11~ "You are worthy, our
Lord and God, to receive glory and honor and
power, for you created all things, and by your
will they were created and have their being."

~**2 Corinthians 5:20**~ We are therefore
Christ's ambassadors, as though God were
making his appeal through us. We implore
you on Christ's behalf: Be reconciled to God.

Chapter 7

~God's Money you borrowed~

Proverbs 3:9 Honor the LORD with your wealth and with the best part of everything you produce.

All money belongs to God. He has instructed us to give Him the first portion of all of our increase. This is done as an act of love not ritual. We love God and since He has trusted us with His money we are delighted to give Him 10% of every ounce of our monetary increase.

You are to give this money to the church you are a member of. This money is used to build God's kingdom. It is a delight to be able to honor God with the money He has blessed you to receive. Money is needed for everything we use to survive.

It is beneficial to honor God with your money so He can continue to bless you to receive more. God gives us the power to obtain wealth. It is His desire that His children have and manage His money according to His kingdom principles.

It is God's plan for His children to live in prosperity. When God's children have abundance you are able to use the money to help those who are in need and fulfill God's plan on earth. God gives us instructions on how to obtain wealth, honor Him with our wealth, give to the needy and give an inheritance to our children's children. We obtain wealth by working. When you get a job it is important to put God's money aside and pay your tithes and offering. You are then responsible for the remaining 90% of your increase to be used wisely.

Always pay your bills on time to establish good credit. Put money aside to pay for your wants in cash. The Bible says we are to owe no man anything except for love (Romans 13:8). The Bible also says that the borrower is a slave to the lender (Proverbs 22:7). You are not to be a slave to anyone except to Jesus Christ.

Don't run yourself crazy by trying to obtain wealth, God knows what you need and has promised to supply ALL your needs according to his riches in glory by Christ Jesus (Philippians 4:19). God knows what you need, and if you submit yourself to Him and follow His commands you will be well taken care of. God owns the world, and gives generously to those who have a heart to receive.

God is not going to give millions to a person who can't manage hundred of dollars. He wants us to follow His principles and become good stewards. This takes time, diligence and discipline in order to manage what God puts in your care. Don't worry God has given you access to His Holy throne to come and ask for wisdom concerning how to be fruitful with what He gives you. (James 1:5 If any of you lacks wisdom, you should ask God, who gives generously to all without finding fault, and it will be given to you.)

It is not God's desire for His children to struggle or to live in poverty. God owns the cattle on a thousand hills (Psalm 50:10), which means He has plenty of resources. God wants to give His resources to His children.

Seek God in what job you should pursue and He will show you how to prosper in your works. God graciously gives His children all things; money is not something God will withhold. God says do your part by honoring Me with ALL your tithes- "And thereby put me to the test, says the Lord of hosts, **if I will not open the windows of heaven for you and pour down for you a blessing until there is no more need.** (Malachi 3:10).

Scriptures

(Romans 13:8), (Proverbs 22:7), (Proverbs 3:9), (Proverbs 19:17), (Luke 6:38), (Matthew 25:14-25), (Genesis 28:20-22), (Matthew 6:25-34), (Psalm 24:1), (2 Thessalonians 3:10), (Acts 20:35), (Proverbs 13:22), (Matthew 6:24), (Deuteronomy 8:18), (Philippians 4:19), (Proverbs 8:18), (Proverbs 28:22), (1 Timothy 6:10), (Luke 6:11), (Ephesians 4:28), (Proverbs 21:20), (Mark 10:23-27), (Deuteronomy 28:11), (Luke 14:28), (Mark 10:29-30), (2 Corinthians 9:8),

(Proverbs 11:4), (Psalm 112:3), (1 Samuel 2:7).

Chapter 8

~Relationship ~ Friendships~

Psalm 1:1 Blessed is the man that walketh not in the counsel of the ungodly, nor standeth in the way of sinners, nor sitteth in the seat of the scornful.

You will have many relationships throughout your lifetime. God loves for you to fellowship with people. It is how you display His love on earth. You have to be cautious about who you spend your time with. Once I gave my life to Christ I literally prayed for godly friends.

God answered my prayers and put me amongst a group of women who love the Lord and inspire me to be my greatest self. This does not mean you walk around with your nose stuck up and survey everyone to see if they love the Lord or not. You have to use wisdom and discernment in deciding who you want to share your life with.

You need people in your corner you can relate with. People who empower you to be better and also hold you accountable. You can determine someone's character by how they act. (Matthew 7:16 You can detect them by the way they act, just as you can identify a tree by its fruit.) The same is true for you. If you want to attract friends of godly moral character you must exhibit godly moral character as well.

You are blessed when you resolve to associate with people who are striving toward following God. They add value to your life, the two of you together can get more accomplished for the kingdom of God. When times are tough you will have someone to encourage you in the ways of God.

You will be able to be each other's support system at various stages in life. God never intended for us to live isolated or to live in constant bickering and confusion. It is God's desire that we live in peace with everyone, because He knows there is power in unity. (1 Corinthians 1:10).

When you associate yourself with a group of individuals your time with them should be meaningful. You have a purpose in life using your time wisely is a necessity. You are here to ignite the fire of God in others and their life should do the same to you. Be kind to everyone and at all times exemplifying God's characteristics.

Friendships/relationships are one of God's greatest blessings. That is why it is important to ONLY give your time to those who honor, respect and love you. Your time is extremely valuable you cannot waste it on dead end relationships. Take your time when you meet new people before you reveal intimate details of your heart. Make sure you

pray and ask God for the intent of the
relationship. God will reveal to you the
meaning of every person that comes into your
life. He will show you if they have good
intentions or if they will be a distraction.
Bless God for the Holy Spirit who guides us
in every aspect of life including friendships.

Remember to always LIVE at peace
with everyone. You will not always agree
with everyone, so disagree in love. When you
need to express how someone has hurt you go
directly to that person and no one else.
(Proverbs 16:28 A dishonest man spreads
strife, and a whisperer separates close
friends.). Be willing to listen to how you may
have offended others as well; being quick to

repent asking God and the person for forgiveness. The goal in life is to glorify God not our emotions. Enjoy the relationships God blesses you to have by loving others the way God loves you.

~1 John 4:7~ Beloved, let us love one another, for love is from God, and whoever loves has been born of God and knows God.

~Proverbs 17:17~ (TLB) A true friend is always loyal, and a brother is born to help in time of need.

~Ecclesiastes 4:9~ Two people are better off than one, for they can help each other succeed.

Scriptures

(Proverbs 4:14-15; 18), (Proverbs 12:15),

(Proverbs 18:24), (Proverbs 27:17), (1

Thessalonians 5:11), (John 15:12-14),

(Proverbs 27:10), (Proverbs 25:17), (Luke

6:31), (Proverbs 11:13), (Matthew 18:20),

(Proverbs 22:24-25), (Amos 3:3), (Romans

12:10-11), (Proverbs 16:23)

Chapter 9

~Surround Yourself with Positive People~

1 Corinthians 15:33 (ESV) Do not be deceived: "Bad company ruins good morals."

Proverbs 13:20 (ESV) Whoever walks with the wise becomes wise, but the companion of fools will suffer harm.

In this life you will be tested when it comes to who you will actually call your friends. When I was growing up I associated with a large group of friends. There was always non-sense brewing within our circle. One week these two were close next week we didn't like each other and the drama kept going full circle.

My mother always told me you would be able to count your true friends on your fingers. What she meant is everyone will not be your friend. As we learned in the last chapter wisdom is the key ingredient when it comes to whom you choose to share your life with.

In some instances you will not be able to control the people who are in your environment. For example, work, school, and who God puts in your family. Your decision to exhibit godly character comes into play when you are in settings like these. You will be required to make a choice to either succumb to how others are acting or be bold and act how God intends for you to act.

It is easy to be influenced by people you spend a lot of time around. God teaches us plain as day by saying DO NOT BE DECIEVED. Deceived means don't trick yourself by thinking you can be around negative influences and it won't have an affect on you- IT WILL.

Guarding your mind, heart and spirit is your responsibility. When you allow God's spirit to teach you and guide you He will keep you from company that is detrimental to your well-being.

Even before I gave my life to Christ I was always attracted to older people. Their wisdom and maturity intrigued me. This doesn't mean age equates to wisdom because there are some old fools and some wise young people.

The Bible is clear when it states, "whoever walks with the wise becomes wise" Proverbs 13:20. Sitting in the company with people who have wisdom will influence you in a positive manner. They will instill what they have learned and be able to offer you beneficial advice on the issues of life. I have a couple of godly mentors who are spiritual mature and aren't afraid to encourage me in the things of God. God will place people in your life to help propel you into your destiny.

Everything God gives adds value to our life. It is no difference when it comes to the company we keep. The latter part of Proverbs 13:20 says, but the companion of fools will suffer harm. Fools will ONLY cause you harm. It's not their fault they can't help it.

They are foolish in their ways and have decided not to follow Christ. If you make a choice to associate with them you run the risk of receiving their foolishness because that is all they know. This may sound harsh but it's the sad truth.

So when you do run into unwise people you need to pray for them and allow God's light to shine through you to influence them to get some wisdom. Association with irrational or unwise people will cause you to suffer harm. Harm is the opposite of what Christ died for on the cross.

Christ came so that you may have life. This life is precious, your time and energy are precious. It is God's will that you enjoy it. Listen to the wisdom, which comes from heaven and use wisdom concerning all aspects of your life.

Chapter 10

~Put God First- Be Bold for Christ~

Romans 1:16 (NIV) For I am not ashamed of the gospel, because it is the power of God that brings salvation to everyone who believes: first to the Jew, then to the Gentile.

People will honor anything they love. God so loved the world that He gave us His only begotten Son, Jesus. The world has it backwards in thinking we have to work at earning God's love. We go through countless attempts to try to earn brownie points from

God when He already loves us. Before you were formed in your mother's womb God knew you and set you apart (Jeremiah 1:5). You are His creation; He loves everything about you. He is only trying to get you to respond to His love.

Once you recognize God's love it will be easy for you to accept it and give Him love in return. It is my prayer for you to experience the love of God in such a way that you know for sure that it is no one else but God himself. God is always present and has been with you every single day of your life. Having your heart conditioned to acknowledge His love is the turning point in your decision making process. Falling in love with God will reconditions your heart to long to be close to Him and to follow His purpose for your life.

Don't ever allow your age to get in the way of your relationship with Christ. Time is not promised to anyone. When you determine in your heart at an early age to surrender your life to Christ you are attaching yourself to the eternal lifeline.

You have joined in with Christ to receive a stream of overflowing blessings to guide your life according to God's plan. His plans are for your benefit. (Jeremiah 29:11 For I know the thoughts that I think toward you, saith the Lord, thoughts of peace, and not of evil, to give you an expected end). God has an entire resource of ways He wants to bless you if you seek His face. Time alone with God is the only way to maximize your relationship with Him and your time on earth.

He is the Creator of all things. He knows All things and wants to give you All things (2 Peter 1:3 His divine power has granted to us all things that pertain to life and godliness, through the knowledge of him who called us to his own glory and excellence,).

Take a look at this verse in the Living Bible translation 2 Peter 1:3-11 *3 For as you know him better, he will give you, through his great power, everything you need for living a truly good life: he even shares his own glory and his own goodness with us! 4 And by that same mighty power he has given us all the other rich and wonderful blessings he promised; for instance, the promise to save us from the lust and rottenness all around us, and to give us his own character. 5 But to obtain these gifts, you need more than faith; you must also work hard to be good, and even that is not enough. For then you must learn to know God better and discover what he wants you to do. 6 Next, learn to put aside your own desires so that you will become patient and godly, gladly letting God have his way with you. 7 This will make possible the next step, which is for you to enjoy other people and to like them, and finally you will grow to love them deeply. 8 The more you go on in this way, the more you will grow strong spiritually and become fruitful and useful to our Lord Jesus Christ. 9 But anyone who fails to go after these additions to faith is blind indeed, or at least very shortsighted and has forgotten that God delivered him from the old life of sin so that now he can live a strong, good life for the Lord. 10 So, dear brothers, work hard to prove that you really are among those God has called and chosen, and then you will never stumble or fall away. 11 And God will open wide the gates of heaven for you to enter into the eternal kingdom of our Lord and Savior Jesus Christ.*

As you look at God's wonderful creations you can vividly see the love of God. It is your reasonable service to submit your life to such a loving Father in order to experience the best life He has predestined for you. Serving God from a heart of worship becomes the norm as you spend more and more time with God.

Spending time with God uncovers His nature. God is able to reveal His characteristics to you and you discover who you really are. God will lead you everyday of your life. As you draw near to Him you will experience indescribable joy. No two days in God's presence are the same; the beauty of God flows as a river that never runs dry.

(John 7:38 He that believeth on me, as the scripture hath said, out of his belly shall flow rivers of living water).

Scriptures

(John 15:16), (Jeremiah 31:3), (Psalm 119), (Colossians 3:4), (Matthew 6:33), (Psalm 42:2), (Psalm 16:11), (Psalm 91:1), (Psalm 23), (Proverbs 16:20), (Deuteronomy 30:19), (Psalm 84:10), (Psalm 139:17), (Psalm 40:5), (Psalm 27:4; 8; 13), (Deuteronomy 6:5), (Luke 12:32), (Galatians 1:10), (Ephesians 1:4), (Galatians 1:10)

Chapter 11

~Prayer: Time alone with God~

1 Thessalonians 5:17 (TLB) Always

keep on praying.

Prayer is communication with God. For some reason people are quick to say pray for me or I am praying for you, but when asked to pray in an open setting they burst out into a sweat. When you pray you are talking to God as your friend, but recognizing Him as Sovereign.

Since the beginning of time God has used communication as the tool for enjoying His creation. He spoke all things into existence. Spending time with God is a delight both for Him and you. God sits in expectation waiting for us to turn and acknowledge Him.

Just think about if you were in a room with someone you were really fond of. You would do everything to get their attention, your heart anticipates them coming over to talk to you. When they finally make the move to engage in conversation with you, your heart is filled with pleasure.

God is the same way, it excites Him when we set aside time to be with Him. Failing to spend time with God through prayer breaks God's heart and hinders us from knowing what to do with our day.

As children of God we have received SO MANY benefits. God has opened His storehouse to pour out an abundance of blessings. We receive these blessing by seeking God first in all things. God knows EVERY day of our life before any of them come to be. He wants to prepare, inform and excite you in the path He has created for you.

The more time you spend with God the deeper you fall in love and the more wisdom you obtain. In God's presence you are free from the cares of the world. His loving nature rejuvenates you as He reveals His beauty.

Prayer is direct access to heaven. We have been given a free will, which means God will not force anything on us. You have to make a choice whether or not you are going to honor God with your time by seeking His face. **Matthew 6:33 But seek ye first the kingdom of God, and his righteousness; and all these things shall be added unto you**.

God is telling you if you come and talk to me and position yourself to receive what I need you to do with your life I will give you the best life has to offer. God is the Master of giving. Everything about His nature incorporates how He wants to bless you. You have the keys to heaven use them. ANYTHING that pertains to life God is concerned about. You can bring all your issues and concerns to God and He will give you hope in return.

Determine in your mind that you will be God's house of prayer. God has so many things He wants to say and reveal to you. Study how Jesus taught His disciple how to pray in Matthew 6. He shows you how to open your prayer with worship, honor and adoration. Next you see what's on the heart of God (His plan is the best).

You must ask the Holy Spirit to guide you in your daily activities. Ask for forgiveness of sin. Then make your supplication known unto God. Always Always Always pray in the Spirit. What I mean by this is you must yield yourself to the prompting of the Holy Spirit. The Holy Spirit will show you how to pray. *(Romans 8:26-27*

TLB 26 And in the same way—by our

faith[a]—the Holy Spirit helps us with our

daily problems and in our praying. For we

don't even know what we should pray for

nor how to pray as we should, but the Holy

Spirit prays for us with such feeling that it

cannot be expressed in words. 27 And the

Father who knows all hearts knows, of

course, what the Spirit is saying as he pleads

for us in harmony with God's own will.)

Pray Always at all times for all

people.

Scriptures

(Colossians 4:2), (Luke 18:1), (Mark 1:35),
(Psalm 92:1-2), (Joshua 1:8), (Luke 16:12), (1
Samuel 1:10), (2 King 6:17), (Job 42:10),
(Daniel 9:4), (Matthew 26:39), (Acts 4:31),
(James 5:15), (Matthew 17:21), (Revelation
5:8), (Ephesians 3:14),
(1 Timothy 2:8), (Matthew 16:19) (Isaiah
56:7), (John 7:29),(2 Chronicles 16:9),
(Jeremiah 29:12), (Genesis 28), (Daniel
10:12), (Galatians 4:6) (Jeremiah 33:3)

Chapter 12

~Wisdom is God's Gift to You~

Proverbs 1:7 Start with God—the first step in learning is bowing down to God; only fools thumb their noses at such wisdom and learning.

Wisdom is a gift from God. God gives you insight concerning every aspect of your life. The first step to obtaining this wisdom is to bow (surrender) yourself to God. Let's think about it God created all things; He knows every day of your life. It is wise to honor Him in worship. As you submit yourself to God He is delighted to teach you how to journey through life. Wisdom is having intelligence and insight and being able to apply it in any given situation to produce the best possible outcome. God loves you so much that He has His hand stretched out toward you willing to give you a wealth of knowledge.

When you make it a point to trust God and follow His instructions you are on the path to a fulfilling life. You will be filled spiritually and naturally. You are able to obtain God's wisdom by reading His word and spending time with Him. As you spend time with God you will develop spiritual insight, which will help you glorify God. Wisdom can be the very difference between you living an unproductive life and the life God has predestined you to have. Wisdom is applied to every piece of your life. One wrong decision can cause your life to go in the wrong direction.

God's wisdom will only lead you on a path of righteousness (right standing with God), which is beneficially to you and the kingdom of God. Today you are without excuse in acquiring wisdom. There are so many avenues to receive the message of hope God is trying to teach you. You have the internet, television, telephone, Bible, church, etc. as tools to hear God's word and instruction on how to live in wisdom on purpose.

Like everything else in life obtaining wisdom is a choice. God pours it out everyday but if you don't drink it, you will not get the nourishment it provides. The bible makes it clear by saying, "only fools thumb their noses at such wisdom and learning" (Proverbs 1:7 MSG). It's foolish to deny the wisdom God is trying to give you by trying to maneuver through life on your own.

When you have God, a Sovereign King of Glory willing to enlighten you in all truth and understanding you accept it. Wisdom is applicable at every stage in life. You need wisdom to do everything. Why not seek the hand of God who created all things and knows the reason in which He created them.

He knows the last day of your life before you were even born. He marks the hand of time and calls all things into existence. God wants to shower you with insight and give your clear guidance.

Loving God with all your heart and trusting Him allows Him to work fully in your life. He wants you to make the right decision every time and prays you yield to Him in order to limit the road of destruction. Will your life be perfect no, because no matter how much we preach wisdom you will not always make the right choice.

It's ok to make mistakes; God's love will draw you back to Him. In that moment you will seek His wisdom and He will show you how to get back on track.

Living a life of wisdom is living a life with God. In His presence He will unveil His plans and purpose to you. As you trust in the Lord with all thine heart; and lean not unto thine own understanding.

In all thy ways acknowledge Him, and He shall direct thy paths (Proverbs 3:5-6) you will experience the best life has to offer. God knows the way in which He is leading you. At every age it is important to stay focused and committed to leaning on God.

He will orchestrate your path and help you fulfill all of your dreams and aspirations. The road travelled will have difficulties but God will show you how to get through them.

God's wisdom teaches you how to deal with everything life throws your way. Keeping you secure in His presence so that nothing will hinder the purpose He placed inside of you.

Scriptures

(James 3:17), (Proverbs 3:5-7), (Deuteronomy 10:12-13), (Proverbs 20:11), (Proverbs 8:32-33), (Lamentations 3:27), (Ecclesiastes 11:9-10; 12:1),

Chapter 13

~Confidence Believe in yourself~

Song of Solomon 4:7 You are

altogether beautiful, my love; there is

no flaw in you.

When you think about how creation came to be, you can visualize God contemplating a vision and then calling things into existence. Once He saw what He created He said, "It was good". After He created both male and female He said, "it was very good" (Genesis 1:27-31). God didn't waste His time in creating you. He loved you from the moment he had the conversation with Jesus and the Holy Spirit about creating man in their own image. You are made to perfection when God looks at you He sees you as your greatest self. Having a relationship with Him will help you to discover your beauty and worth.

To God you are whole and complete. Unfortunately the world's system has tainted the way individuals sees themselves. In the world beauty is determined by size, outward appearance and credentials. In God's eyes your very existence makes you flawless.

Psalm 139 13-14 For you formed my inward parts; you knitted me together in my mother's womb.14 I praise you, for I am fearfully and wonderfully made. Wonderful

are your works; my soul knows it very well.

God wants you to know without a shadow of doubt how much He loves you. As you were being created in your mother's womb God was gloating at the sight of His wonderful creation. He knows how special you are and wants you to realize it as well.

Once you grasp hold of how God sees you, false implications will begin to fade away. You will no longer have a need for validation, because your confidence will be established in God. You'll be able to look in the mirror and say I am "Fearfully and wonderfully made." God took His time in making me just the way He wanted me to be.

Although you may have weaknesses as we all do they will not hinder you or destroy your self-confidence. Building your self-assurance will come from believing in yourself. God thinks so highly of you; your thoughts ought to parallel to His.

One rule of thumb I learned long ago was to believe ONLY what God says about me. *(Colossians 1:22 he has now reconciled in his body of flesh by his death, in order to present you holy and blameless and above reproach before him,)*. Life will try to tare you down by making you think you are not worthy of God's love. If you can't remember anything else remember His love. God loves you so much that Jesus became a sacrificial offering just for you.

Jesus died on the cross, an unpleasant death in order to present you as holy, blameless and without fault. So whenever you feel your self-esteem wavering which it will- remember how much God loves you. He is never far away.

In those moments of feeling inadequate as if you were in the world all alone go to the Father. Make a determination to use the only remedy that works- trusting God. God didn't give us instructions as a suggestion He knows what you need to be whole and complete in Him.

God did not create you to shift back

and forth in your emotions. He wants you to know you are His beloved child. Your mind is your greatest weapon in living a confident life.

(Romans 12:2 GW Don't become like the people of this world. Instead, ***change the way you think.*** Then you will always be able to determine what God really wants—what is good, pleasing, and perfect.) Your confidence is filtered by the way you think of yourself and whether or not you believe what God thinks about you.

God tells us plainly not to be like the people in the world who allow their mind to shift like the wind. Instead allow God to renew your mind daily –then you will know and understand what pleases God. It pleases God when you think well of yourself. When you think well of yourself you are in alignment with God.

You agree that His creation (You) is a magnificent extension of Him. God does everything with divine intention- surely you being created was on purpose. Think the way God thinks about you and live free!

2 Corinthians 10:4-5 (For the weapons of our warfare are not carnal, but mighty through God to the pulling down of strong holds;)5 Casting down imaginations, and every high thing that exalteth itself against the knowledge of God, and bringing into captivity every thought to the obedience of

Christ;

Chapter 14

~Child of A King~

1 John 1:12-13 But to all who believed him and accepted him, he gave the right to become children of God. 13 They are reborn—not with a physical birth resulting from human passion or plan, but a birth that comes from God.

God is your Father you have been called into His kingdom as His child. Once you believe and accept Jesus you are adopted into God's glorious family. God's family is perfect. The way He loves and cares for you is beyond your wildest imagination. Before you can even form your lips to require of Him He is already there with an answer (Isaiah 65:24). Being in God's family is a great gift.

As your Father He promises to take care of you. Every need of yours is met in Him. Beyond the natural and physical blessings you receive from God there is an eternal blessing. God has given you access to dwell with Him as His child forever.

When you die you will go and live with Him and bask in His glorious splendor FOREVER. Jesus became your living hope. He gave you the Holy Spirit to assure you of the things to come. Everyday of your life should be lived in expectation of living with God forever.

Knowing you are a child of a King you have to line up with your citizenship, which is in heaven. A citizen represents the country from which it belongs. You are God's representatives in the earth. You receive all of your commands from heaven.

Everyday when you wake up you should turn to God to receive the assignment He has for you. As a child of God you embody the characteristics of Jesus Christ. The same mind that was in Christ is now in you. Jesus has given you the Holy Spirit to help you know and understand how to function as a kingdom citizen. This will only be done through an intimate and continuous relationship with God.

As a child of God you have been given access to EVERY spiritual blessing in heavenly places (Ephesian 1:3). This means as far as it pertains to blessings you have received every possible form of blessing there is. As God's elite children you have been granted eternal (they never run out) blessings.

You are a joint heir with Christ Jesus. You receive from God the very glory Christ had when He walked the earth. An heir is a beneficiary; you are a recipient of the essence of God's kingdom. In order to walk in the fullness of God's kingdom you have to allow His Spirit to guide you. God's spirit knows the ways of God's kingdom. He will reveal to you how to conduct yourself in a manner that represents God well. Like Jesus you have to set your mind on heavenly things. Your attitude has to be inspired by knowing who you are in Christ. In everything you do you must reflect the loving nature of your Father.

Romans 8:14 GW Certainly, all who are guided by God's Spirit are God's children Ephesians 1:3 Blessed be the God and Father of our Lord Jesus Christ, who has blessed us in Christ with every spiritual blessing in the heavenly places,

Scriptures

(Ephesians 2:19), (Philippians 3:20),

(Galatians 3:26), (Romans 8)

(Colossians 1:19; 3:1-4), (Matthew 7:11)

Chapter 15

~Don't be afraid -You are Never Alone~

Joshua 1:7-9 (NIV) "Be strong and very courageous. Be careful to obey all the law my servant Moses gave you; do not turn from it to the right or to the left, that you may be successful wherever you go. 8 Keep this Book of the Law always on your lips; meditate on it day and night, so that you may be careful to do everything written in it. Then you

will be prosperous and successful.

9 Have I not commanded you? Be

strong and courageous. Do not be

afraid; do not be discouraged, for the

Lord your God will be with you

wherever you go."

God gives clear instructions on how to remain strong and courageous. Why do you think God would imply such a command? The answer is because He knew circumstances and people would try to place fear on you.

Fear is an unfriendly feeling caused by considering something bad is going to take place. First you must know God did not give this emotion to you. Fear came about because of a disconnection from God.

In order to remain fearless you have to stay before God and allow Him to control your emotions. (Numbers 6:26). God wants you to live in a place of peace EVERYDAY. This is why He tells you to be strong and Very courageous. God is never far away. He resides on the inside of you.

The more time you spend with God the more you begin to understand His virtue and characteristics. You were not created to walk in fear.

In 1 John 4:18 God tells you fear involves punishment. His perfect love cast out fear. You have been given the Mighty strength of God to walk through life free from being scared of what life may throw your way. Being strong and courageous is easy to say. There will be times in your life where you will feel overwhelmed and fear may set in. In those moments God is telling you not to succumb to overwhelming emotions but to fall into His hands of grace. God is for you; His number one desire is for you to enjoy the life He had graciously given You.

Being afraid is a trick of the enemy to try to get you off the course God has predestined you for. When you walk in fear you become paralyzed you aren't able to accomplish much of anything. Your mind begins to fill up with thoughts like, "I won't make it", "Life isn't worth it", "Why is this happening to me. " God doesn't care". Trust me I have been there. This is not the mind of Christ.

Just think about it- Jesus knew before He came to earth that He was going to die a gruesome death. He saw His entire human life before it happened. Yet, when He came He fulfilled what God wanted Him to accomplish. Don't you think everyday when He woke up He considered the pain He would have to endure. Although He knew the discomfort He would face He kept His eyes on God (Hebrews 12:2-4). You must keep your eyes on Jesus. After all God said, "Be strong and courageous. Do not be afraid; do not be discouraged, for the Lord your God will be with you wherever you go."

God is everywhere at all times and He longs to help you. Do not be discouraged on days when you can't seem to control your emotions or when nothing seems to be going your way. You must rely on God's Word as your weapon to counteract fear.

Whatever is causing you to feel inadequate search God's word pertaining to your situation and speak it into the atmosphere. This will get you into alignment with the promises of God. God watches over

His word to perform it Jeremiah 1:12. This is why He tells you to mediate in the word day and night. In these moments praise God. Thank Him for allowing you to go through a little piece of what Jesus went through.

Worship will draw you close to God and diminish all negative thoughts. God will cause your mind to reposition itself properly. You were created to worship. This is were you surrender your heart, mind, soul and Spirit to give adoration to God.

Thank God for the good days that give you rest, and thank Him for the bad days that stretch your faith. As you grow in God continue to put your trust in Him. When difficulty arises give it to God. He is equipped to handle it; put your focus on loving God and obeying Him. He will do the rest.

Scriptures

(Psalm 23), (Ephesians 6:17), (Jeremiah 1:12), (2 Timothy 1:7), (Psalm 91), (Hebrews 13:5), (Romans 12:12), (Deuteronomy 31:6-8), (1 John 4:4), (Matthew 5:45), (Hebrews 12), (Isaiah 41:18:43:19), (Psalm 107:35)

Chapter 16

~Love yourself~

1 Corinthians 13:4-7 4 Love is patient and kind; love does not envy or boast; it is not arrogant 5 or rude. It does not insist on its own way; it is not irritable or resentful; 6 it does not rejoice at wrongdoing, but rejoices with the truth. 7 Love bears all things, believes all things, hopes all things, endures all things.

In order to properly love the world around you, you must love yourself. God shows us perfect love by giving you an illustration in 1 Corinthians 13. This teaches you how God loves, how to love yourself, and how to love others. First you must be patient and kind. Often times we are our worst critique.

If something goes wrong you automatically blame yourself. God is merciful He wants you to be patient with yourself. You can not get everything right all the time. He uses your mistakes to show you His awesome power. Being patient is a great tool for self-control. God doesn't want you to do anything on impulse. Being patient will allow you to seek God First in all circumstances. Kindness is a characteristic God wants you to practice as well.

You should care about yourself and your future. Every day you should seek God for the plans for your life. Your obedience to God sets the course for everyone attached to you.

When you love yourself you are careful to watch what goes into your spirit. The bible says, "Guard your heart above all else, for it determines the course of your life" Proverbs 4:23. Whatever you allow to enter your heart will determine the course of your life. You can't allow bitterness, hatred, discord, hurt, pain, confusion, and etc. rest in your heart.

God's Spirit lives in your heart.

You have to make room for Him so He can properly function inside of you. Loving yourself will cause you to make decisions that are pleasing to God. What pleases God will also please you. Ultimately loving yourself is an expression of gratitude toward God. You are saying, "Thank You God". You are pleased with the way God created you and take care of yourself so you can be a reflection of Him in the earth.

God loves you more than words can express. His love flows like a river that can't be contaminated. As you bask in His glory you radiate His splendor in the earth for others to experience as well. God is all you

will ever need. Listen for His voice every day.
Be in constant communion with Him. Receive
His knowledge and experience the ways of
God.

Scriptures

(Galatians 2:20), (1 Corinthians 13:4-7),
(Mark 12:30), (1 John 4:16), (Matthew 16:24-
25), (John 15:2), (Philippians 2:3), (Genesis
1:26), (Romans 5:8) Psalm 112:1-2

Stay in Contact with Nicole Atkinson

Website: www.nicoleatkinsoninc.com

Email: nicoleatkinsoninc@gmail.com

Facebook personal page:
https://www.facebook.com/nicole.atkinson.980

Facebook community page:
https://www.facebook.com/Nicoleatkinsoninc?fref=ts

Instagram: nicoleatkinsoninc

Sybia,
May you walk with God always. You are the apple of His eye. Walk with God always.

Love,

Made in the USA
Charleston, SC
19 May 2015